# The Future Begins with the Past

## An Archives Exhibit of Jewish Rochester

Phyllis Kasdin
The Jewish Community Center
of Greater Rochester

Fossil Press
Rochester, New York

The Future Begins with the Past: An Archives Exhibit of Jewish Rochester
Phyllis Kasdin
Jewish Community Center of Greater Rochester

Published by
Fossil Press
100 Parkwood Avenue
Rochester, New York 14620

Distributed by
Jewish Community Center of Greater Rochester
1200 Edgewood Avenue
Rochester, New York 14618

Printed in the U. S. by ColorCentric Corporation, Rochester, New York
ISBN 978-0-9770986-0-6

# Contents

# Foreword

While it is still possible to call up warm memories of the "world of our fathers," Rochester's Jews are to be commended for this graphic memoir of their community's past. Their story provides a noteworthy chapter in the annals of American Jewry.

Historian Abraham J. Karp, who served in this city for 35 years as rabbi and professor, discusses in his books how Jews in America sought haven and found home. His last book, *Jewish Continuity in America*, describes the "Americanization" of Congregation Beth Israel in Rochester, New York, depicting "creative survival in a free society." Rabbi Karp writes:

> *America extended freedom and offered equality which permitted Jews to establish their communal identity and the institutions that sustained it. A network of organizations and institutions labored at integrating immigrant Jews into the economic, social and cultural fabric of the larger community.*

In these pages are reflected the movements and tensions, as well as the triumphs, that engaged communities throughout America. The early and later immigrations, the conflict between assimilatory tendencies and the desire to maintain their precious religio-ethnic heritage, the eventual overcoming of social prejudices so that Jews could become leaders in education and culture—all are clearly seen. Beyond the similarities to other cities, there are areas where Rochester excelled, such as pioneering prominence in the clothing industry, attainments in higher education, and devotion to synagogue, philanthropy, and the perpetuation of Jewish tradition, helped by remarkable rabbis and communal leaders.

> *The experience of the Jew in America serves to instruct how one group has striven to fulfill its dual and complementary commitment to the political society and to its own religio-cultural-ethnic group, with both grace and integrity.*

The story of Rochester's people, of its pioneers and heroes in personal and public life, continues to inspire.

**Deborah Karp,**
*wife of the late Rabbi Abraham Karp, spiritual leader of Temple Beth El for 16 years, is an author, lecturer, and teacher. She now resides in New York City.*

*"Phyllis Kasdin, staff coordinator for 'The Future Begins With The Past: An Archives Exhibit of Jewish Rochester' at the Jewish Community Center, looks through some Miller's soda bottles on display in the exhibit. Photo by Annette Lein."* This photograph and caption were printed in Rochester's Democrat and Chronicle *newspaper on November 21, 2004, on page 4C, as an illustration for a feature article by Stuart Low about the exhibit, entitled "On the Street Where They Lived."*

# Preface

For the past 25 years I have been collecting memorabilia of Jewish Rochester for the Jewish Community Center. As a native Rochesterian, this had become a labor of love. In the spring of 2004, I decided it was time to share these precious items with the Rochester community. I assembled a committee of dedicated individuals who worked diligently sorting and categorizing the collection. By early November the exhibit, "The Future Begins with the Past," was ready for display in the lobby of the Jewish Community Center.

The excitement generated by this exhibit exceeded my wildest expectations. For people harboring memories of long ago, particularly of Joseph Avenue, the center of Jewish life in Rochester at the time, this was a "trip down memory lane." For those who were not native Rochesterians and for those too young to remember, the exhibit proved to be a valuable history lesson about Jewish Rochester.

Hundreds of people came to the JCC to view the exhibit. Many made repeat visits. Those who viewed the exhibit sent its catalog to relatives and friends who once lived in Rochester. I received many long-distance requests for copies of pictures and the exhibit catalog.

The popularity and excitement generated by the exhibit inspired us to create this book, *The Future Begins with the Past*. It has been an honor working on it. I hope you will enjoy it as much as I have enjoyed the process of bringing life to our memories.

*Phyllis Kasdin*
*Rochester, New York*
*June 2005*

(The photographs and memorabilia included in this book were taken from the JCC archives, and from individuals who offered items from their collections. We realize that it is not all-inclusive. Also, if something that was displayed in the original exhibit does not appear in the book it is only because of space limitations.)

# Acknowledgements

This book became a reality because of the creativity, encouragement and support of many people.

Special thanks to all those who shared their collections of early Jewish Rochester with us: Eileen and Michael Grossman, Anne Korenstein, Mordecai Kolko, Muriel and Sam Katz, Ruth Lempert, Eleanor Lang, Tillie Levinson, Arnold Gissen, Albert Newman, Leonard Sonders, Diane Rock, Temple Beth El, Sol Goldstein, Cynthia Goldstein, Lois DeCoste and the Weinstein family, Irving Germanow, Leonard Simon, Gilbert Cresov, Naomi Silver, and Will Greenberg and Judith Lurie, archivists at the Jewish Home.

Our deepest gratitude goes out to Michael Peres who generously gave of his time and expertise to photograph and prepare the pictures for the book. Without his enthusiasm for this project, this book would not have become a reality. It has been an honor and a privilege working with Frank and Patricia Cost, designers of the book. Their creativity and dedication to making this book the very best it could be is most appreciated. And many thanks to Deborah Karp for writing the Foreword to this book, and to Karin Kasdin for editing and proofreading portions of it.

We are deeply appreciative of the support and generosity of our underwriters: the Joseph and Anna Gartner Foundation Philanthropic Fund (Carol and Michael Hirsch); the Brodsky-Grossman Supporting Foundation, Inc. (Alan Brodsky, Eileen and Michael Grossman, Betsey and Marc Haas, and Lisa and Andrew Curwin); the Stephen Rosenberg Memorial Fund (Haskell, Sunny and Nellie Rosenberg); Seymour Fogel; and Josephine and Simon Braitman. Our heartfelt thanks for helping to make our dream a reality.

Our exhibit, The Future Begins with the Past, took many, many hours and great dedication from the exhibit committee who sorted, cataloged, and created the displays for the archives. Many thanks to Leon and Millie Berman, Rose Bresloff, Joshua Bruner, Rochelle Cresov, Helen Hecker, Carol Hirsh, Muriel and Sam Katz, Elliott Landsman, Ruth Lempert, Howard LeVant, Tillie Levinson, Muriel Oratz, Ory Pranger, Irving Ruderman, Eugene Salesin, Jeannette Schwartz, Millie Tanenbaum, and Joanne Viener for all they did.

For access to the 1926 map of the Joseph Avenue area, thanks go to Larry Naukum, head of the Local History Division, Central Library of Rochester and Monroe County, New York. We are also most appreciative of Sheila Kaplan for her administrative support and for keeping us on task.

A special thanks to Carol and Michael Hirsh for their encouragement, enthusiasm and generosity.

Phyllis Kasdin

# The Future Begins with the Past

*Gabriel Wile was one of the first Jewish settlers in Rochester. He and his partner Myer Greentree established the first tailoring shop in Rochester. The firm Greentree and Wile is recognized as the parent of Rochester's men's clothing industry. The Wile tombstone is located in Mount Hope Cemetery.*

# History of the Rochester Jewish Community

THE HISTORY of the Rochester Jewish community parallels that of most cities in the United States. Jewish people immigrated to America along with people of other faiths and shared in the general economic, social, political and cultural evolution of our country. As they settled in new and different cities, the Jews worked diligently to maintain and even enrich their religious and cultural heritage by developing traditional communal institutions. Jewish immigrants to Rochester adjusted to their new environment fairly quickly and soon began to make significant contributions to the economic life of Rochester. The Jews played a major role in the economic transformation of the city of Rochester from an industrial city relying almost exclusively on flour mills to a major clothing manufacturing center.

The first Jews to arrive in Rochester were of German descent. Myer Greentree, a peddler, was one of the first to settle in Rochester around 1843. He soon gave up peddling and became an employee of Sigmund Rosenberg's dry goods store. Rosenberg was another of the very first Jews to settle in Rochester. Greentree married a non-Jewish woman and soon took over a children's clothing manufacturing shop that his wife had been operating on Front Street. Around 1848, Greentree was joined by three other Jewish newcomers, Joseph and Gabriel Wile and Hirsh Britenstool, and the shop became Rochester's first large-scale clothing manufacturer.

This firm, Greentree and Wile, is recognized as the parent of Rochester's men's clothing industry.

Slowly other Jewish men, some with their wives, settled in Rochester. By 1850 there were approximately sixty Jews living here. Many started working as peddlers, but before long became clerks, grocers, jewelers or, more frequently, clothing merchants. These new settlers were anxious to succeed and worked very hard. Their labors were rewarded and by 1850 at least half of Rochester's Jews were identified with local clothing manufacturing. Small tailor shops opened along Main Street and, by 1860, there were 42 shops. At this point, many shop owners began to form partnerships and consolidate their businesses. These businesses became the leading clothing firms in the Northeast.

The Jewish clothing industry thrived during the Civil War. By the end of the war the Jews were firmly entrenched in the community, but, as Jews, could not fully participate in neighborhood social life. Sometime before 1868, the first Jewish social club was founded. The social and economic position of the Jews in 1870 was a far cry from their plight just two decades earlier. In 20 years, they had succeeded in becoming Rochester's fourth largest ethnic group, and leaders in its industrial, political, and civic life.

# Synagogues

The emergence of Jewish religious life is characterized by the organization of a congregation and the establishment of a Jewish burial ground. In 1848 a plot of land in Mount Hope cemetery was purchased by three prominent Jews. At the same time, informal religious meetings were held, probably in people's homes. Soon this congregation moved to a hall on Front Street. The *hazzan* was the leader of the congregation in prayer as well as the preacher and teacher. The congregation, known then as the Front Street Synagogue, recognized the need for a rabbi to preach and educate. Rabbi Tuska was hired and conducted the congregation along traditional lines. As time went on, several different rabbis were employed to lead the congregation, which had been named "Berith Kodesh." There was dissension among the more traditional members and those who advocated eliminating outdated ritual, wanting to follow the pattern of Reform synagogues in Germany.

From its very first days, this congregation faced the problem of caring for Jews in financial need. It founded the Hebrew Benevolent Society to function as the synagogue's welfare department. Those active in the synagogue were also active in the Hebrew Benevolent Society. In many ways, this synagogue became the core of the Jewish community.

Eastern European Jews started to migrate to Rochester towards the end of the 19th century. Berith Kodesh was not a traditional enough synagogue for this group, and, in fact, the congregation was not anxious to have them as members. These new immigrants asserted their own identity by purchasing their own burial ground and establishing Beth Israel, their own congregation. Dissension arose among some of the members of Beth Israel, which led to the formation of other Orthodox synagogues in the vicinity of Joseph Avenue. By the time of Urban Renewal in the 1950s there were 20 Orthodox synagogues in the Joseph Avenue area.

By 1910 many Orthodox congregations in other cities were shaping their religious and educational programs along lines that were later recognized as characteristic of Conservative Judaism. The Conservative movement was committed to traditional Judaism, and also desired to be in harmony with the demands of American life.

The younger and wealthier members of Beth Israel, or the "Leopold Street Shul," as it came to be called, were beginning to move into the eastern part of the city. As the Jewish population grew around the East Avenue/Park Avenue area, the residents wanted to establish a congregation closer to their homes. This group of younger Beth Israel members was dissatisfied with transplanted Eastern European Orthodoxy, yet they were unable to adjust to Reform Judaism. Their response was to establish Temple Beth El as the Conservative congregation of Rochester. Soon after Temple Beth El's incorporation, the Park Avenue Baptist Church at the corner of Park Avenue and Meigs Street became available for purchase. Temple Beth El purchased it for $45,000 and held its first services there on Passover in 1917. The Temple Beth El congregation grew rapidly as more Eastern European Jews became affluent and moved to the eastern part of the city. By the early 1950s it became evident that the congregation had outgrown its Park Avenue building. Land was purchased on the corner of Hillside Avenue and Winton Road and a school, administrative offices and an auditorium were built. High Holy Day services were held in both the Park Avenue building and the auditorium of the Winton Road facility. On Saturday, January 23, 1960, a fire broke out in the Park Avenue Temple and completely destroyed the facility. This tragedy became the impetus to add a sanctuary to the already existing edifice on Winton Road. The sanctuary was dedicated in June 1963.

By the turn of the century, Berith Kodesh shortened its name to B'rith Kodesh. With the ever increasing numbers of Eastern European Jewish immigrants and the establishment of a number of other Orthodox synagogues, B'rith Kodesh was no longer the leading synagogue in Rochester. Interest in synagogue life was waning and in an attempt to revitalize it, Friday evening services were abolished and the major service of the week was held on Sunday. In a short time, further attempts were made to change the traditional habits that still remained. Holidays, with the exception of Rosh Hashanah, Yom Kippur, Passover and Shavouth, were celebrated on the nearest Sunday. Bar Mitzvot were abolished, very little Hebrew was included in the service, and the rabbi officiated at intermarriages. This radical change in doctrine did not increase interest in religious life as was hoped.

Rabbi Horace J. Wolf became senior rabbi of Temple B'rith Kodesh in 1910. He found a pulpit rich in the tradition of community service and radical in its ritual pattern, and a congregation with little interest in religious pursuits. The Reform congregation had moved away from traditional Jewish life, and in the process, lost contact with the non-German Jewish groups in the city. Rabbi Wolf infused new life into his congregation. He helped to strengthen the Sunday school and opened it to children from the Orthodox community. Under Rabbi Wolf's leadership, the Orthodox and Reform communities reconciled. Relationships improved between the German and Orthodox groups. Rabbi Horace Wolf was one of the fathers of Rochester's Jewish community.

In 1925, Rabbi Philip Bernstein took over the pulpit at Temple B'rith Kodesh. He was born in Rochester to Eastern European Orthodox parents. The atmosphere of the Rochester Jewish community began to change in 1925. Although a better understanding developed between the Orthodox and Reform groups, the synagogue as an institution became a weaker link in the chain of community life. As a result, new Jewish agencies and movements developed in response to the evolving needs of the growing Jewish community.

*Dr. Max Landsberg came to Rochester with his wife from Germany to become the spiritual leader of Temple Berith Kodesh in 1871. Soon after his arrival in Rochester, Dr. Landsberg began to introduce reforms. He changed the prayer book to one that had no prayers in Hebrew, allowed men to worship without head coverings, abolished Bar Mitzvot, approved intermarriage, and attempted to move as close to Christian practices as the congregation would tolerate.*

Beth Israel Synagogue, commonly known as the "Leopold Street Shul," was the first Orthodox synagogue in Rochester. It was established in 1867 by early Eastern European immigrants who could not give up their traditional ways and thus could not identify with Reform services and practices at Temple Berith Kodesh.

Congregation Ahavas Achim Anshei Radishowitz, commonly known as the "Rhine Street Shul," was established by immigrants not wishing to worship in synagogues already established by the earlier immigrants. In 1892 they built their own synagogue on Rhine Street near Hudson Avenue. Eventually this congregation attracted a large number of tailors and in 1896 became known as the "Congregation of Tailors," or the Chevra Chayteem.

*Temple B'rith Kodesh on the corner of Gibbs Street and Grove Street, circa 1925. Temple Berith Kodesh was the first synagogue to be established in Rochester. The few Jews who lived in Rochester in the mid-1800s first met in people's homes and then in a small building on Front Street. The early congregants were primarily German Jews who were accustomed to Reform services. After renting space in the Baptist Church on St. Paul Street and Andrews Street for one year, the leaders of the congregation were able to purchase the building and worshiped there for 40 years. Then, because of the commercialization of the area, it was decided that it was no longer suitable for a synagogue. The new home for Temple Berith Kodesh on Gibbs Street was dedicated in June 1894. Several years later, its name was shortened to B'rith Kodesh. By the 1950s the Gibbs Street facility could no longer accommodate all the congregants for High Holy Day services, making it necessary to hold these services in the Eastman Theater.*

*The "Kipeler Shul" on Ormond Street, its original location.*

*The "Kipeler Shul" on Joseph Avenue after the move.*

ROLLING ALONG — Orthodox Jewish synagogue in unorthodox situation reels down Joseph Avenue en route to new site at 703 Joseph. Congregation Ahavas Achim Kipel Volin had been at 472 Ormond St. until yesterday, but had to move because of redevelopment project. It was last of nine Orthodox synagogues to leave area, and had many observers on its precarious trip.

*Turning the "Kipeler Shul" to face east, after moving it down Joseph Avenue, August 24, 1961.*

As a result of Urban Renewal in the 1950s, the synagogues on Hanover Street, Ormond Street and Rhine Street were demolished. The members of Ahavas Achim Anshel Kipel Volin, or the "Kipeler Shul," as it was commonly called, opted to move their house of worship rather than destroy it. The building was moved down Joseph Avenue to its new location across the street from Congregation B'nai Israel. Because worshipers must face east while praying, the building was turned around so that the arc faced east.

*The curtain that once covered the arc containing the holy Torot at Ahavas Achim Anshel Kipel Volin, commonly known as the "Kipeler Shul."*

*This clock designated the time of daily services at the "Kipeler Shul."*

*Greggor used on Purim at the "Kipeler Shul,"* rubber stamp for the Kipeler Linas Hazadek, *and box that once housed Chanukah candles.*

9

*The Nusbaum family established its own synagogue on Ormond Street, Beth Hakneses Hachodosh, commonly known as the "Nusbaum Shul." When this house of worship (pictured above) was demolished during Urban Renewal in the 1950s, the congregation purchased what once was a church on St. Regis Drive in Brighton, and it became the second Orthodox synagogue in the area. It is a flourishing and vibrant congregation today.*

Sephardic Jews came to Rochester from Yugoslavia and Greece. Their language was Ladino, a form of Spanish. The Sephardic immigrants established their own synagogue, Light of Israel, on Hanover Street. Because their synagogue building was demolished during Urban Renewal, the congregation built a new synagogue on Norton Street, and worshiped there for many years. As the neighborhood changed and the congregants moved away, Light of Israel was sold. The Sephardic Community has always been very close-knit, and rather than abandon their roots the congregants worship today in a designated area of Congregation Beth Shalom.

*Beth Hamedresh Hagadol, or the "Big Shul" as it was commonly known, was located on Hanover Street. It was not only the largest but also the most beautiful Orthodox synagogue in the area. On High Holy Days, throngs of worshipers would congregate on the grand stairway leading to the entrance. The synagogue was demolished in the 1950s to make room for Urban Renewal. The members of the "Big Shul" and the "Leopold Street Shul" joined together to form a Conservative congregation, Beth Hamedresh Beth Israel, now located on the corner of East Avenue and Hawthorne Street.*

*"Big Shul" Choir. It was not uncommon for the Orthodox synagogues to have children as part of their choir on High Holy Days. In the 1950s, Beth Hamedresh Hagadol, the "Big Shul," enlisted young boys to participate in its choir. The boys featured in the photograph were from Rabbi Abraham Solomon's "Cheder."*

13

*Breaking ground for Beth Joseph Center. In the late 1930s it became apparent that an Orthodox synagogue was needed in the northern part of the city. Ground-breaking for this beautiful new Shul took place in 1939. Beth Joseph Center was a vibrant synagogue through the 1940s, '50s and '60s. As the neighborhood changed and the Jews moved away, the synagogue disbanded. Those congregants who remained joined other synagogues.*

*Plaque honoring the memory of Harry Susman for his many years of dedicated service to Beth Joseph Center.*

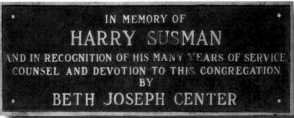

IN MEMORY OF
**HARRY SUSMAN**
AND IN RECOGNITION OF HIS MANY YEARS OF SERVICE
COUNSEL AND DEVOTION TO THIS CONGREGATION
BY
**BETH JOSEPH CENTER**

*Confirmation picture of the class of 1947 at Beth Joseph Center. Featured in the picture are (back row) Donald Silverman, Mordecai Kolko, Michael Silverberg, Stanley Fisher, Carl Voldman, Melvyn Kost, (second row) Gloria Wolf, Alyne Rappaport Phillips, Joan Lee Markus, Margo Rosbach, Sylvia Adler, Joanne Susman Viener, (seated) Phyllis Schwartz Kasdin, Jerome B. Gordon, Rabbi Leon Stitskin, Carol Fritt Lee. Photo by Samuel W. Bloom.*

*Exterior of Temple Beth El on Park Avenue and Meigs Street after the fire.*

Temple Beth El, the first Conservative synagogue in Rochester, made its home on the corner of Meigs Street and Park Avenue. The main building housed a sanctuary and reception hall, and the religious school was located in a building next door. In the early morning hours of January 23, 1960, a fire broke out in the Meigs Street building. The building was destroyed, but miraculously the Torot and other sacred objects were saved. The photograph to the right shows the interior of the temple shortly after the fire. As a result of the fire, all Temple Beth El operations moved to the corner of Winton Road and Hillside Avenue. Photos by Eugene Edwards.

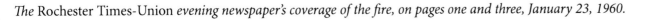

*The* Rochester Times-Union *evening newspaper's coverage of the fire, on pages one and three, January 23, 1960.*

Congregation B'nai Israel Ahavas Achim is the only surviving synagogue in the Joseph Avenue area. The congregation was established by immigrants from Austria and thus was originally known as the "Austrian Shul." The synagogue pictured here (built in 1928) is now referred to as the "Joseph Avenue Shul." Rabbi Henry Hyman, the congregation's spiritual leader, conducts services on the Sabbath and on holidays. Photo by Frank Cost.

As the Jewish population moved to the southeast end of Rochester and to Brighton, it became apparent that a new location for Temple B'rith Kodesh in Brighton was a necessity. Consequently groundbreaking for a new building on Elmwood Avenue that would meet the needs of the congregation took place in 1962. Today, Temple B'rith Kodesh is a dynamic and vibrant Reform congregation that attracts thousands of congregants on the High Holy Days.

# Organizations and Institutions

The early settlers in Rochester were German Jews who assimilated quickly into the mainstream of life even though a chasm existed between them and the non-Jewish community. The influx of Eastern European Jews to Rochester troubled these early settlers. They did not speak of this publicly, but it became apparent when the German Jews found themselves living side by side with new immigrants from Poland and Russia. It did not take long for them to move away from Chatham, Joiner and Oregon Streets, where the newcomers settled, to the more desirable neighborhoods of Union Street, East Avenue, and streets off these main thoroughfares.

Although the German Jews did not socialize with the new immigrants, much of their philanthropy was directed towards them. Living conditions among the newcomers were poor. They lived in old houses and their large families crowded the few bare rooms they could afford to rent. To help supplement the family income, young boys worked in the "newspaper business." Jewish immigrant boys hawked their newspapers throughout the city. These newsboys, many of whom became successful business and professional men, established relationships that lasted well into adulthood.

Large numbers of Russian and Polish Jews continued to arrive in Rochester. Most of them were poor. Many, unable to speak English, became peddlers and made a meager living. Conditions were especially difficult in the winter months. Despite the fact that the German Jewish community had a long history of organized relief work in the community, the Russian and Polish Jews felt the need to organize their own charitable enterprise known as the "United Jewish Charities." Around the same time, local leaders of the wider immigrant community came to believe that it would be necessary to combine major relief activities into a single federation.

Three organizations, the Talmud Torah, Hachnosas Orchim and the Hebrew Ladies Relief Society, joined forces and incorporated as the "Associated Hebrew Charities." The purpose of the Associated Hebrew Charities was to furnish temporary assistance to those in distress and to provide free Hebrew education to poor Jewish children. By 1920, the Associated Hebrew Charities became a modern social service agency. Since its mission was humanitarian rather than ideological, all segments of the Yiddish-speaking community cooperated and supported it. The Charities provided a sense of community on an organizational level that had not before existed.

Because the Rochester Community Chest (the forerunner of the United Way) saw no reason to subsidize both the United Jewish Charities and the Associated Hebrew Charities, these two groups merged and became the Jewish Welfare Council.

At the turn of the century, most Rochester Jewish immigrants found employment as tailors, cutters, trimmers, pressers, and spongers in the clothing industry. They worked long hours for meager pay. Sharing a common plight, some of the workers united and periodically went on strike. Although most of these strikes proved ineffective, the group decided to become the Socialist Labor Party. In 1903, in order to further Socialist ideology, 23 of the more radical clothing industry workers organized a branch of the "Arbeiter Ring," called the "Workmen's Circle."

Members of the Workmen's Circle were considered radical and sacrilegious. They had little regard for the Sabbath, holding lectures on Friday nights. These lectures, conducted in Yiddish, were particularly appealing to the new immigrants. The Progressive Library, established by the Workmen's Circle at the corner of Baden and

Chatham Streets, attracted a wide and eager reading public.

The plight of the Jews in Europe and the desire for a Jewish homeland in Palestine was of great concern and interest to these Eastern European immigrants. The German Reform Jews whose allegiance was to their native or adoptive country, not to Zion, did not share this concern. Nevertheless, a Zionist movement started in Rochester, and in 1914 the 17th national convention was held here. This convention had a great influence on many Russian and Polish immigrants, increasing the support for Zionism in Rochester. At the convention, the women's organization Daughters of Zion changed its name to Hadassah.

Concern for the plight of the clothing industry workers and the great desire for a Jewish homeland in Palestine led to the organization of the "Poale Zion" or Labor Zionists. The group flourished and soon was able to purchase its own home at 27 Buchan Park. An afternoon school opened in which both Yiddish and Hebrew were taught. They organized a credit union offering small loans at low interest. The Poale Zion was the only Zionist group that owned its own home in Rochester and that conducted intensive educational and cultural activities.

As early as 1877, the Jewish Orphan Asylum of Western New York was located in Rochester on North St. Paul Street. It later moved to a large house on the Genesee River gorge. The Jewish Orphan Asylum of Western New York continued to house children who were being raised in the Reform tradition until 1928. It was considered unsatisfactory, however, for children from traditional homes. In 1912, the Jewish Sheltering Home was founded, and in 1914 opened its doors at 27 Gorham Street to six Orthodox Jewish children. In 1919, Jacob

Hollander became the superintendent. Under his care the organization maintained strictly Orthodox practices and it flourished. Two volunteer auxiliaries were formed: the Mother's Club and the Big Brothers and Sisters Club. Members of these clubs worked to ensure that the resident children enjoyed celebrating birthdays and other special events. By 1921, the Jewish Sheltering Home had outgrown the original building at 27 Gorham Street. Cottages were added, making a total of five buildings able to accommodate up to 100 children. Because some mistakenly believed that older people were also living there, the Jewish Sheltering Home changed its name to the Jewish Children's Home.

As the Jewish population aged, the need for an institution to care for older people became apparent. In 1918, a home purchased at 1162 St. Paul Street was converted into the Jewish Home for the Aged and operated according to Orthodox rules and regulations. Many in the German-Jewish community were affluent enough to afford private nursing care and had little need for such an institution. Over the years, however, the Jewish Home for the Aged expanded to accommodate a growing elderly population. Ultimately, in 1985 a new facility opened its doors on Winton Road.

Because the Americanization of the Eastern European immigrants became a great concern for the earlier German-Jewish settlers, plans for a settlement house on Baden Street were initiated in 1901. The Baden Street Settlement opened its doors in 1904 primarily to teach immigrant women about sanitation, cooking, and housekeeping. The Settlement also served as a recreational, educational and health center for Jewish children and adults.

# Announcement

Rabbi Hyman B. Faskowitz       Rochester Vaad Hakashruth

It is with deep regret that we inform you the Jewish Community of Rochester that after a thorough investigation we have discovered that many of you have been misled by unscrupulous butchers and poultry dealers who sold poultry as kosher when the kashruth of the poultry was in serious doubt.

In order to prevent this practice in the future and to protect he Jewish community, it has been decided to institute the following procedure.

ANY POULTRY WHICH YOU PURCHASE THROUGH A BUTCHER OR DEALER MUST BEAR THE STAMP OF THE ROCHESTER VAAD HAKASHRUTH.

> R. V. H.
> KOSHER

THIS STAMP IS YOUR ASSURANCE THAT THE POULTRY WAS SLAUGHTERED IN ACCORDANCE WITH JEWISH LAW.

Any poultry NOT BEARING THIS STAMP signifies that it was not slaughtered properly and therefore is "TREIF" and unfit for use in Jewish homes.

The Vaad Hakashruth assumes no responsibility for any poultry which does not bear the stamp.

To check on the reliability of your butcher or dealer we recommend that you contact our Rabbi – Rabbi Hyman B. Faskowitz at 32 Morris Street – HAmilton 3290.

Help us assure proper community supervision by co-operating with your Vaad Hakashruth representing all of Rochester's Synagogues.

**ROCHESTER VAAD HAKASHRUTH**

FRIDAY, JANUARY 1, 1954

---

In view of the fact that the **M. LAPIDES MEAT MARKET** of 461 Joseph Ave., **MISLED** the public **BY OFFERING NON-KOSHER** meats for **KOSHER:**

**WE HEREBY DECLARE** that according to the Jewish law, **LAPIDES MEAT MARKET LOST HIS RELIABILITY TO HANDLE KOSHER** meats any more.

We therefore let the public know that this meat market is **NO LONGER UNDER OUR SUPERVISION** and we are **NOT RESPONSIBLE** for the Kashruth of the meats and poultry purchased there.

# ROCHESTER VAAD HAKASHRUTH

HYMAN B. FASKOWITZ, RABBI

*Rochester Vaad Hakashruth announcements. The Vaad Hakashruth, or the "Vaad" as it is commonly called, consists of a group of rabbis knowledgeable in the rules of ritual slaughter as well as other elements of kashruth. There was often a great deal of dissension among the butchers and the Vaad. The Vaad had the authority to designate a butcher un-kosher and thus posted notices in synagogues discouraging people from patronizing these butchers.*

The Poale Zion or Labor Zionist Organization, a left wing of the Zionist movement advocating the Marxist-Zionist ideology, grew when the Balfour Declaration of 1917 was announced. They could now afford to purchase their own home on Buchan Park.

*Signage from the Labor Zionist building on Buchan Park.*

*Members of the Poale Zion, or Labor Zionists, in 1920 in their new home on Buchan Park.*

23

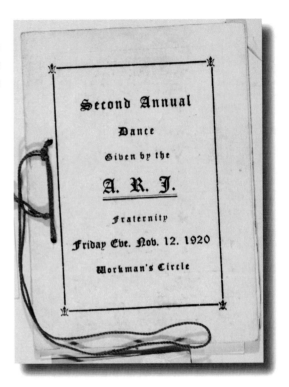

*A 1920 dance program from the Workman's Circle fraternity.*

In 1903, a branch of the "Arbeiter Ring" called the "Workmen's Circle" was organized in Rochester in order to propagate the Socialist ideal among Jewish workers. This composite photograph shows the makeup of the group in 1925. Photo by Jaffeson.

*The B'nai Zion Hebrew Library was organized in 1901 using four rooms leased over a bakery on the corner of Chatham Street and Baden Street. A few years later they moved to 14 Chatham Street, and in 1916 to 52 Chatham Street. The new building featured an auditorium that sat 150. Many lectures and meetings were held there. It also housed a lending library of Yiddish, Hebrew and German Books. This certificate is the official charter of the library.*

*In 1921 a house was purchased at 1162 St. Paul Street and converted into the Jewish Home for the Aged.*

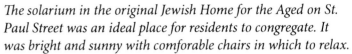

The solarium in the original Jewish Home for the Aged on St. Paul Street was an ideal place for residents to congregate. It was bright and sunny with comforable chairs in which to relax.

The Jewish Home for the Aged followed strict kashruth laws. The Daughters' Club prepared the meals served in the dining room.

The bedrooms in the original Jewish Home for the Aged on St. Paul Street were small and bare. Nevertheless, residents often socialized in each other's rooms.

The residents of the Jewish Home were mainly Orthodox. (Witness all the men wearing kipot.) Card playing was a great pastime for some of the men.

By the early 1940s it became apparent that the Jewish Home for the Aged needed to be expanded to accommodate the increasing number of residents. Rabbi Leon Stitskin (fourth from the right) of Beth Joseph Center, the Home's next door neighbor, officiated at the 1949 dedication of the cornerstone for the addition.

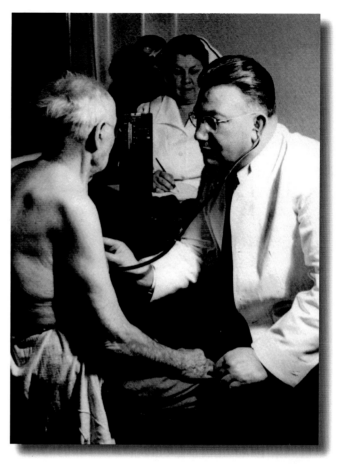

Dr. William S. Ruben examining a patient at the Jewish Home. Dr. Ruben had a practice in general medicine on St. Paul Street.

*The Rochester Jewish Relief Society was organized to help Jews in need. This photograph is from 1934.*

*Trophy awarded to winners of the Jewish Relief campaign, September 28, 1917. The team consisted of Hyman Kolko, captain, Harris Nusbaum, Philip Nievert, Abraham Kolko, Jacob Gordon, David Neimkin, Lesser Paley, Moses Cohen and Gus Kaminsky. From the collection of Mordecai Kolko.*

JEWISH ORPHAN ASYLUM—ROCHESTER, N. Y.

*In 1877 a group of men and women joined together to form the original Jewish Orphan Asylum, which eventually came to be located on Genesee Street. Its religious ideology followed the radical Reform movement. Orphaned children from Buffalo and Syracuse also lived there.*

The Jewish Children's Home on Gorham Street was originally called the Jewish Sheltering Home. The name was changed to the Jewish Children's Home because some mistakenly believed that the home also housed adults. Although there was already an orphan asylum on land along the Genesee River gorge, it was felt that as a Reform-sponsored orphan asylum, it was not a satisfactory place to send Orthodox children. The Gorham Street home was strictly Orthodox in every way. In 1919 Jacob Hollander, a native of Jerusalem, became superintendent and remained in that position until the Jewish Children's Home closed in the late 1940s. Some of the children who lived at the Gorham Street home are pictured below and on the facing page.

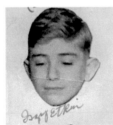

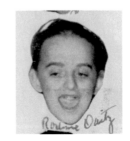
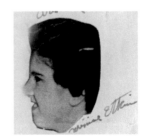

30

*The Jewish Children's Home at 27 Gorham Street in Rochester was supervised by Jacob Hollander. Mr. Hollander wanted his children to be "good" Americans, and so becoming a boy scout or a girl scout was mandatory.*

HAROLD GOLDBLATT

Vera Berman

SAM ITKIN

MORTON HOLLANDER

*These photographs and those on the preceding pages of children who lived at the Jewish Children's Home were reproduced from a collage board that the children made as a tribute to Mr. Alfred Hart, a great benefactor of the Home.*

*This photograph of the board of directors of the Jewish Children's Home on Gorham Street was taken in the late 1930s. The portrait on the wall behind the group is of Alfred Hart, a great benefactor of the Home and a former member of the board. He lived in a mansion on East Avenue, and often invited the children to his home for dinner with his family. His widow, Mrs. Ida Hart, is seated in the center of the group. She remained on the board and continued her husband's work. Mr. Hollander, superintendent of the Jewish Children's Home, is standing behind her, directly under the portrait of Mr. Hart.*

33

*Charter of the Jewish War Veterans of the United States, David J. Kauffman Post, No. 41, June 1, 1932.*

## Jewish Young Men's and Women's Association

In 1895, a cultural group known as the Judean Club was established with the help of Rabbi Paul Chertoff of the "Leopold Street Shul." Rabbi Chertoff was a great influence on the younger men of his congregation, and helped to shape the future leadership of the Rochester Jewish Community. Among the members of the club was Philip Bernstein, who later became chief rabbi of Temple B'rith Kodesh.

While most boys in the Judean Club were mainly interested in intellectual pursuits, others were interested in athletics. Mr. Alfred Hart recognized the need for a facility where the boys could enjoy both cultural and athletic activities. In 1907, the Jewish Young Men's Association was established and, soon after, the Jewish Young Women's Association was established, and a building on Franklin Square was purchased. This facility served the Jewish young people well, although a survey, conducted by the National Jewish Welfare Board, deemed the Franklin Square building and its limited scope of activities inadequate.

In 1929, a one million dollar building fund campaign was held. The campaign, surpassing its one million dollar goal, laid the groundwork for the Andrews Street building. The facility was designed to house educational, physical, and recreational activities, with the upper four floors reserved for resident dormitories. Construction began and the outer walls were erected. Unfortunately, the Depression also began, and donors were unable to pay their pledges. There were not enough funds to complete the project. The building stood

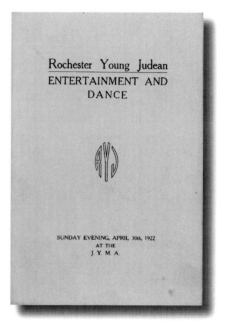

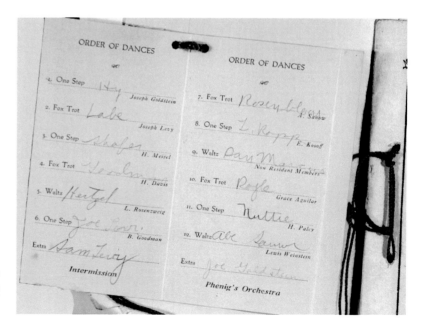

*In the 1920s and 1930s, dance cards were very popular at social functions. Each boy and girl was issued a card listing dance partners for the evening.*

as an outer shell from 1931–1935, when a great community-wide drive was held to raise the $200,000 needed to complete it. With the support of the non-Jewish community, the Jewish Young Men's and Women's Association building on Andrews Street was completed and dedicated in 1936. Before long, the myriad cultural, physical, educational and social activities taking place at the JY made it the center of the Jewish community.

Some JY social functions combined several activities in one evening. This program from May 23, 1926 is for a play entitled His Children by Rufus Learsi, followed by a social hour and dance.

*The first home of the Jewish Young Men's Association, organized in 1908, was located at 3 Franklin Square. The Judean Club was the forerunner of the first JY. A variety of social, cultural and recreational activities were conducted in the 18-room building. Subsequently it became apparent that more space for additional programs was needed. A new structure was added in 1912 that included a combined auditorium and gymnasium and a small pool. Photo by Osband Studio.*

JY on Andrews Street. By 1929, the Jewish Young Men's and Women's Association building on Franklin Square was no longer adequate to meet the needs of the Jewish Community. A very successful building campaign was held and the groundwork for the Andrews Street Building was laid. The outer walls were erected but because of the Depression work had to stop for lack of funds. With the help of the Rochester community, another successful building fund campaign was held and the Andrews Street Building was completed and dedicated in 1936. It became a popular meeting place for all ages in the Jewish comunity. The first three floors contained meeting rooms, a large auditorium/theater, bowling alley, gym, pool, locker rooms, health clubs, lounges, game rooms, and a restaurant. The upper floors were devoted to resident dormitory rooms for men.

The Jewish Ledger's *coverage of the laying of the cornerstone for the Andrews Street Jewish Young Men's and Women's Association building (JYM&WA), May 29, 1931.*

*A closer view of the front doors of the new JY on Andrews Street. While the building date on the stone to the right of the doors is 1931, the building was actually completed in mid-1936.*

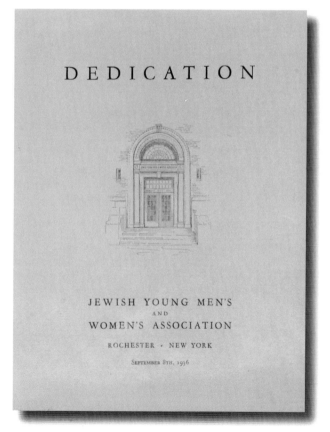

*Program for the dedication of the opening of the new JY, September 8, 1936.*

*Alpha Thoma Strata. Some young men who did not join existing fraternities formed their own fraternity and named it Alpha Thoma Strata, "Greek" for "off of Thomas Street." It was one of the original fraternities at the Andrews Street building. First row seated: Sidney Monson, Phil Cilman, Max Springut, Milton Komenski, Harold Shapiro. Second row: Buddy Baker, Morris Fink, Dave Sanders, Sol Goldstein, Mike Weiner, Eli Gilbert, Manny Rosen, Mike Umansky, Bernard Shapiro, Sam Rockowitz, Garson Cilman, Izzy Cherry, Seymour Lippman, and Manny Hirsch. From the collection of Sol Goldstein.*

*The Theta Phi Kappa's cast for a 1931 operetta in drag production. Back row, left to right: Mort Rycin, Al Goldman, Chuck Schwartz, Dave Margolis, Leon Berman. Center row: Fred Kravetz, Stanley Marcus, Oscar Karch. Front row: Garson Salin, Sidney Cuan, Jim Itkin, Harry Stoler, and Sam Baron. Photo by S. Stanton Singer.*

# The Fratority News

### "Official News Bulletin of Rochester's Fraternities and Sororities"

VOL. 1—NO. 1     MAY 4, 1936     FIVE CENTS

## Association Building To Open

### DEDICATION

The publishers of "The Fratority News" dedicate its initial issue to the numerous sororities and fraternities throughout the city of Rochester and we sincerely hope that you will find keen enjoyment within its pages.

With this enterprise we hope to increase the mutual feeling of cooperation and interest that exists between your organizations. We hope you will look to "The Fratority News" as a source of information and interesting publications concerning your friends.

We shall make every effort to promote your interest. Constructive criticism will be duly appreciated.

THE PUBLISHERS

### Facilities Provided For Group Meetings

With the near opening of the new JYMA building all fraternities, sororities, and clubs, are eagerly awaiting to view the new meeting rooms which the association directors have so generously set aside for their use.

The rooms, which are equipped with all the modern conveniences that can be desired, are located on the third floor and will be kept open at all times.

At present the following clubs will be privileged with the using of these club rooms: Theta Phi Kappa, Supremes, Eta Beta Phi, Jays, Tru-Pals, Alpha Thoma Strata, Palisons, Kappa Beta Rho, Marvelettes, Sub-Debs, Alomos Club, and the Eta Sigma Gamma.

A great number of new fraternities and sororities will undoubtedly move in at the new building to enjoy the privileges extended to them.

The directors of the association have been and will be in the future, working hand in hand with the clubs and their guidance has helped ward the success that has been attained. They have planned a varied program to stimulate interest and the clubs are indeed honored to have outsiders take such an interest in them.

The numerous clubs of the YMCA, Brick Church Institute, CYMA, and many other organizations in Rochester work with the clubs giving them a guiding hand whenever called on.

### Comments

To the Editor:

After one of your representatives called at our meeting informing us that a fraternity and sorority news publication was to be published, we held an informal discussion in connection with it.

It has created quite a bit of enthusiasm among the fellows and on behalf of the club I offer you my congratulations and good luck in your very interesting "Fratority News."

Fraternally yours,

A Theta Phi Kappa Member.

Dear Sir:

On behalf of my sorority I write you this letter wishing you success in the "Fratority News."

We all feel that with the average cooperation from the organizations the "Fratority News" shall create enough interest and enjoyment that we will all look forward to each and every issue.

Again I offer you my best wishes in hoping that the "Fratority News" will be a part of every active fraternity and sorority in the City of Rochester.

Sincerely yours,

A Alpha Sigma Phi Member.

The Sigma Lambda Alpha Sorority, Junior Chapter, is making plans for a Mothers' Day Party to be held on May 17 at Green Gables. Dorothy Geldin is chairman of the affair with Ida Slater and Shirley Sklof assisting.

A regular meeting of the Sigma Alpha Sorority was held at the home of Miss Susan Sisler April 16.

Mail all subscriptions and news to "FRATORITY NEWS" 36 O. K. Terrace on or before May 15.

*From the 1930s to the 1960s, high school fraternities and sororities were very popular in Rochester. Some of them met at the JY. The May 4, 1936 issue of* The Fratority News *(above) announced the opening of the new JY on Andrews Street.*

HOWARD SENZEL

STUART SPECTOR

ROBERT LOVENHEIM

# SIGMA TAU OMICRON SWEETHEART BOOK COMMITTEE

## FEBRUARY 18, 1961

HARVEY ROSEN

VARDEN STUDIO

ROBERT CROOG

*A page from the 1961 Sweetheart Booster Book of the Sigma Tau Omicron Fraternity.*

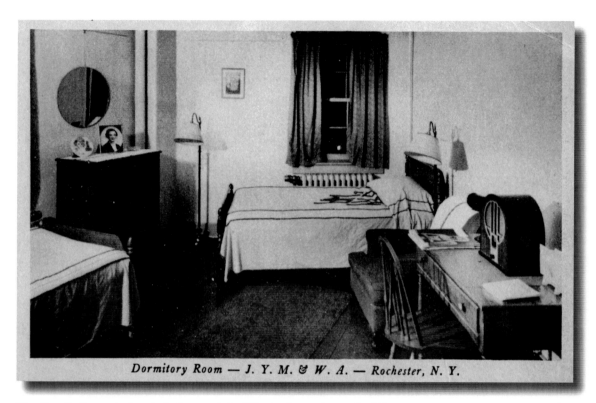

Dormitory Room — *J. Y. M. & W. A.* — Rochester, N. Y.

The fourth through the sixth floors of the JY's Andrews Street Building were dedicated to dormitory rooms for men. Many men staying in Rochester for a short period of time utilized these rooms. There were also some single men who made the JY their home on a permanent basis.

Soup plate, dormitory key, and stamp of incorporation for the Jewish Young Men's and Women's Association on Andrews Street.

A Few of the Varied Activities at the Jewish Young Men's & Women's Association

(Left to right) Miss Ruth Carson, Miss Florence Greenhouse, Miss Sylvia Schwartz and Miss Etta Kotpeck are members of the Intermediate Girls Group of the JYWA who will appear in a specialty dance number in the minstrel show tomorrow evening for the benefit of the girls' summer camp.

*From the late 1920s through the early 1940s, yearly minstrel shows were presented in the auditorium of the JY. The stage at the JY at that time was one of the best equipped in the city. Some of Rochester's "Rockettes" are featured above.*

*A collage of newspaper photographs featuring the varied activities available at the new JY on Andrews Street served as a promotion for the second annual membership drive in the late 1930s.*

# "CAMPUS MUSIC"

A
Musical Comedy

Presented By

**THE JY MINSTRELS**

Saturday and Sunday
April 22 and 23, 1939

⟨All Proceeds to be Used for Scholarship Fund⟩

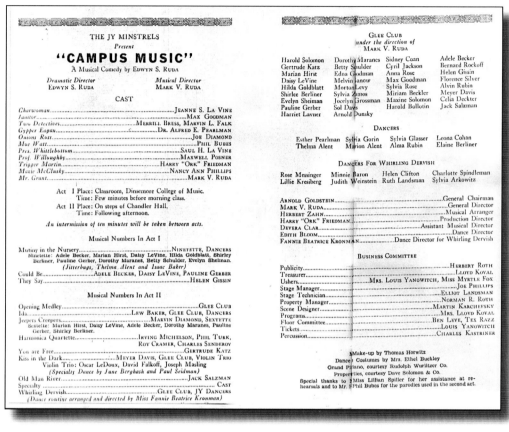

THE JY MINSTRELS
*Present*
**"CAMPUS MUSIC"**
A Musical Comedy by EDWYN S. RUDA

| Dramatic Director | Musical Director |
|---|---|
| EDWYN S. RUDA | MARK V. RUDA |

CAST

Charwoman.................................................JEANNE S. LA VINE
Janitor.......................................................MAX GOODMAN
Two Detectives................MERRILL BRESS, MARVIN L. FALK
Gypper Eagan...........................DR. ALFRED E. PEARLMAN
Onions Ross...............................................JOE DIAMOND
Moe Watt....................................................PHIL BUBES
Pres. Whittlebottom..............................SAUL H. LA VINE
Prof. Willoughby....................................MAXWELL POSNER
Trigger Martin.......................HARRY "ORK" FRIEDMAN
Maxie McClusky...........................NANCY ANN PHILLIPS
Mr. Grant..................................................MARK V. RUDA

Act I  Place: Classroom, Dinsemore College of Music.
Time: Few minutes before morning class.
Act II Place: On steps of Chandler Hall.
Time: Following afternoon.

*An intermission of ten minutes will be taken between acts.*

Musical Numbers In Act I

Mutiny in the Nursery.................NINETETTE, DANCERS
Ninetette: Adele Becker, Marian Hirst, Daisy LeVine, Hilda Goldblatt, Shirley Berliner, Pauline Gerber, Dorothy Maranes, Betty Schulder, Evelyn Sheiman.
(Jitterbugs, Thelma Alent and Isaac Baker)
Could Be..........ADELE BECKER, DAISY LEVINE, PAULINE GERBER
They Say....................................................HELEN GISSIN

Musical Numbers In Act II

Opening Medley...........................................GLEE CLUB
Ida.....................LEW BAKER, GLEE CLUB, DANCERS
Jeepers Creepers..................MARVIN DIAMOND, SEXTETTE
Sextette: Marian Hirst, Daisy LeVine, Adele Becker, Dorothy Maranes, Pauline Gerber, Shirley Berliner.
Harmonica Quartette.................IRVING MICHELSON, PHIL TURK,
ROY CRAMER, CHARLES SENDEROV
You are Free...........................................GERTRUDE KATZ
Kiss in the Dark.........MEYER DAVIS, GLEE CLUB, VIOLIN TRIO
Violin Trio: Oscar LeDoux, David Falkoff, Joseph Masling
(Specialty Dance by June Berghash and Paul Seidman)
Old Man River..........................................JACK SALZMAN
Specialty........................................................CAST
Whirling Dervish.................GLEE CLUB, JY DANCERS
(Dance routine arranged and directed by Miss Fannie Beatrice Kronman)

GLEE CLUB
*under the direction of*
MARK V. RUDA

| | | | |
|---|---|---|---|
| Harold Solomon | Dorothy Maranes | Sidney Coan | Adele Becker |
| Gertrude Katz | Betty Schulder | Cyril Jackson | Bernard Rockoff |
| Marian Hirst | Edna Godman | Anna Rose | Helen Gissin |
| Daisy LeVine | Melvin Janow | Max Goodman | Florence Silver |
| Hilda Goldblatt | Morton Levy | Sylvia Rose | Alvin Rubin |
| Shirlee Berliner | Sylvia Zimos | Miriam Beckler | Meyer Davis |
| Evelyn Sheiman | Jocelyn Grossman | Maxine Solomon | Celia Deckter |
| Pauline Gerber | Sol Davis | Harold Bollotin | Jack Salzman |
| Harriet Lavner | Arnold Dunsky | | |

DANCERS

| | | | |
|---|---|---|---|
| Esther Pearlman | Sylvia Gorin | Sylvia Glasser | Leona Cohan |
| Thelma Alent | Marion Alent | Alma Rubin | Elaine Berliner |

DANCERS FOR WHIRLING DERVISH

| | | | |
|---|---|---|---|
| Rose Messinger | Minnie Baron | Helen Clifton | Charlotte Spindleman |
| Lillie Kresiberg | Judith Weinstein | Ruth Landsman | Sylvia Arkowitz |

ARNOLD GOLDSTEIN.........................................General Chairman
MARK V. RUDA.................................................General Director
HERBERT ZAHN.................................................Musical Arranger
HARRY "ORK" FRIEDMAN.............................Production Director
DEVERA CLAR.........................................Assistant Musical Director
EDITH BLOOM....................................................Dance Director
FANNIE BEATRICE KRONMAN......Dance Director for Whirling Dervish

BUSINESS COMMITTEE

Publicity.........................................................HERBERT ROTH
Treasurer...........................................................LLOYD KOVAL
Ushers..................MRS. LOUIS YANOWITCH, MISS MYRTLE FOX
Stage Manager.....................................................JOE PHILLIPS
Stage Technician............................................ELLIOT LANDSMAN
Property Manager..........................................NORMAN R. ROTH
Scene Designer.........................................MARTIN KARCHEFSKY
Programs..................................................MRS. LLOYD KOVAL
Floor Committee..........................................BEN LEVE, TEX RAZZ
Tickets.....................................................LOUIS YANOWITCH
Percussion................................................CHARLES KASTRINER

Make-up by Thomas Horwitz
Dance Costumes by Mrs. Ethel Buckley
Grand Piano, courtesy Rudolph Wurlitzer Co.
Properties, courtesy Dave Solomon & Co.
Special thanks to Miss Lillian Spiller for her assistance at rehearsals and to Mr. Phil Bubes for the parodies used in the second act.

*Another successful minstrel show, "Campus Music," was written and directed by Mark V. and Edwyn S. Ruda in 1939. The Ruda brothers were the driving force behind almost all of these minstrel shows. They wrote, directed and produced them.*

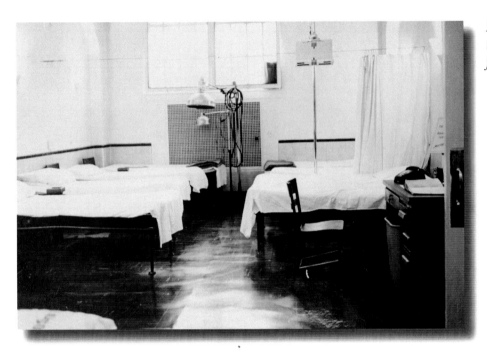

*Massage room at the JY. Men who belonged to the Health Club were able to receive a massage from Red Shapiro.*

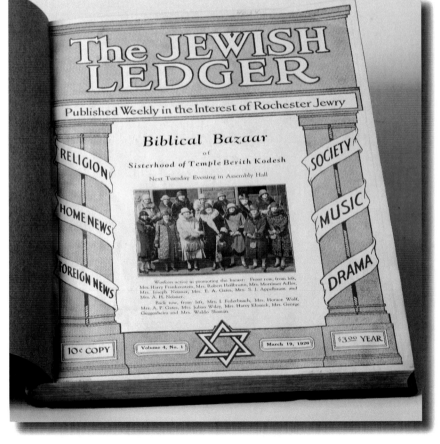

*Bound book of* Jewish Ledgers *from the year 1926. The Jewish Ledger is the oldest and now the only Jewish newspaper in Rochester. It was started in 1924 as an activity of the Jewish Young Men's Association.*

MEMBERS OF THE ARMED FORCES
*Welcome to*

USO

ROCHESTER'S USO CLUB
123 FRANKLIN SQUARE          MAIN 5971
*All Services and Facilities Free*
Lodging, Light Meals, Showers, Lounges
Shaving and Pressing Equipment
Music and Recreation Rooms   Home Hospitality
Personal Counseling, Library, Writing Rooms
Music Rooms, Table Games—Ping Pong, Billiards
Dancing and Hostesses, "Talk a Letter Home"
Outdoor Recreation

21

*During World War II, the Franklin Square building was turned into a USO for Jewish Servicemen. It was a place where servicemen could come to relax and socialize with members of the Rochester Jewish community.*

*This card catalog of Jewish servicemen who fought in World War II was kept at the JY building on Andrews Street.*

## Camps

Jewish camping programs became important in the mid-1920s. The JY's first overnight camp was Camp Conesus, the forerunner to Camp Seneca Lake. Camp Sisol, housed in the Andrews Street building, became a popular day camp. As the demand for day camps grew, the need for an outdoor facility became apparent. Land was purchased in Mendon and Markus Park became a popular place, not only for children attending Camp Sisol, but also for the general JY membership who enjoyed the outdoor pool.

*Camp Conesus was the first overnight camp sponsored by the JY. Located on Conesus Lake, the camp was first opened for boys only, but later incorporated girls. This photograph is from 1930.*

*Camp Seneca Lake staff and campers, July 11, 1945. Camp Seneca Lake has become one of the foremost Jewish resident camps in the Northeast part of the country.*

*A baseball game at Camp Seneca Lake in the early 1950s. Ronald Axelrod is running to first base.*

*Camp Seneca Lake's dining hall was also a multipurpose room for many years.*

# JYMA *Campers*

A pictorial trip through the J. Y. M. A. Camp on Conesus Lake just above Lakeville where the Jewish boys can play more, eat more and sleep more in a 24-hour-day than they ever before thought possible.
Stone Photo

An exciting game of volley-ball, with the speed of tennis, the skill of basketball and a lot of fun all rolled in together.

J. Y. M. A. Camp Councillors assembled in front of their executive tent. Front row, left to right: Al Rabin, athletics; Robert Baker, head councillor; Aaron Rose, camp director; Samuel Feld, Indian lore. Standing: Morton Rubin, Swimming; Herman Levine, hiking and boating; Edgar Present, assistant head councillor.

The old-fashioned boy who "just whittled" with his pocket knife has been succeeded by the craft worker and in this camp some very good work has been turned out by the

*This newspaper article is from Rochester's Democrat and Chronicle of August 21, 1932. It highlights some of the campers and activities at Camp Conesus.*

*Camp Sisol staff, 1938. Camp Sisol was originally housed in the Andrews Street JY building. Children had the use of all the facilities, including the pool and the solarium off the Lodge Room on the third floor.*

Camp Sisol, named after two important leaders of the JY, Simon Stein and Sol Heumann, is still a vibrant day camp. Today it is located at Markus Park, the JCC's summer facility in Mendon, New York.

## Jewish Community Center of Greater Rochester

As the neighborhood surrounding the JY changed and the Jewish population migrated south to Brighton and north to Irondequoit, it became apparent that a new facility was needed in the suburbs. A building committee was established and after searching for a building location, the kind offer by Max Farash of 20 acres on Edgewood Avenue was accepted. With the move to Edgewood Avenue, the Jewish Young Men's and Women's Association's name (JY) was changed to the Jewish Community Center of Greater Rochester (JCC). Neither the move nor the name change altered the mission of the JY. The new building provided even greater opportunities for physical education, the arts, early childhood activities, senior adult programming, Jewish programming, and a wide variety of other programs established to meet the needs of the community. In April of 2001, as a result of the vision and generosity of Louis Wolk, the Wolk Children's Center opened on the JCC grounds. This state-of-the-art facility houses a child care center and nursery school.

*Ground-breaking for the Jewish Community Center on Edgewood Avenue took place in 1969. The photo features Herman Shukovsky, then executive director, Morris Shapiro, Ida Hart, Irving Germanow, David Gray and Irving Ruderman.*

*By the 1960s it became apparent that the JY building on Andrews Street was not meeting the needs of the Jewish Community. The majority of the Jewish people now lived in the southeast end of the city and in Brighton. Land on Edgewood Avenue was acquired from Max Farash and the Jewish Community Center of Greater Rochester was built and opened its doors in 1973. Building chairpeople were Samuel Poze and Sanford Liebschutz. Left to right standing: Joseph Kaplan, Joseph Goldstein, Samuel Kolko, William Konar. Seated: Mrs. Julia Belore, Mrs. Phyllis Kasdin, and Mrs. Gertrude Weider.*

When the Holocaust Survivors living in Rochester became comfortable with their new life in America, they felt the need to reconnect with family members that had perished during this terrible time. Under the leadership of Rabbi Abraham Karp, Hazzan Samuel Rosenbaum and Leonard Freedman, then executive director of the Jewish Community Center, a Holocaust Commission was established to construct a Holocaust Memorial in the courtyard of the JCC. David Klass of New York City was commissioned to design and craft the memorial. It was unveiled and dedicated during the Yom Hashoah service in 1982. A Wall of Remembrance that includes the names of family members of Rochester's survivors who perished during the Holocaust was erected in 1991.

*Yom Hashoah (Holocaust Remembrance Day) service in 1977.*

*Dedication of the Holocaust Memorial at the Jewish Community Center in 1982. Rabbi Abraham Karp is at the podium, and Michael Moszkowicz (in his concentration camp clothing) is standing to his right.*

# Sports

At the turn of the 20th century, basketball became the most popular sport for Jewish boys, and the first addition to the JYMA was a gym to accommodate the sport. Many Jewish boys who were introduced to basketball at the JY became outstanding players, and subsequently played on their high school teams. The Washington Playground located behind Washington High School provided another venue both for basketball and baseball. When the Andrews Street building opened in the late 1930s, women also became involved in athletic pursuits. Volleyball and swimming were very popular for women.

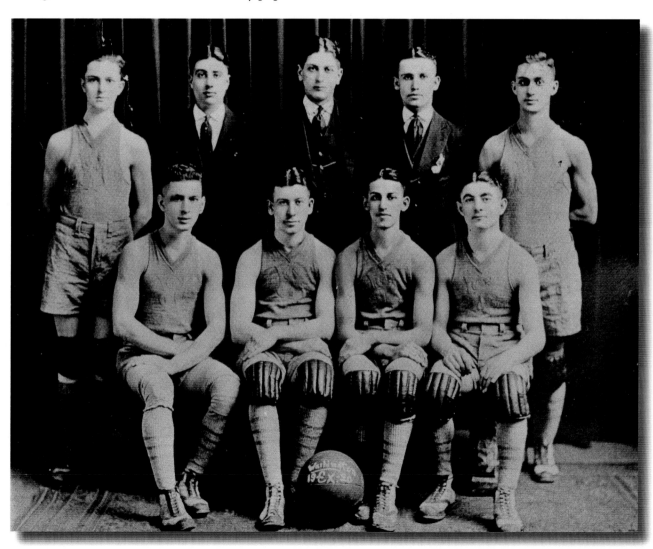

*The Washington Playground Basketball Team of 1920. Washington playground, located behind Washington High School, was a popular place for boys in the area to play basketball.*

*Les Harrison (center), a graduate of East High School, became the manager of the Rochester Royals basketball team, nationally recognized in the 1940s and 1950s as one of the most successful teams in the country. Photo from the late 1940s.*

*JY Women's Volleyball. Volleyball was very popular among the young women at the JY. The team not only played in volleyball tournaments, but as a group held many social events at the JY.*

*Handball was very popular at the JY. The men featured in this 1955 photograph are: (standing, left to right) Bello Snyder, Leo Simpson, Hy Olshan, Lou Karpell, Dave Sachs, Mike Weiner, Jerry Cohen, Mike Bobby, Morrie Whitaker, (seated) Jap Apperman, Manny Hirsch, Harry Wolfe, and Kay Dickman.*

*The EJICO'S (pronounced Chico's) swim team of the JY was composed mainly of boys from the Sephardic Community.*

# Schools

The first priority for immigrant parents was to provide both a Jewish and American education for their children. Jewish children attended public school during the day and Hebrew school or "Cheder" after school and on Sunday mornings. School Number 9, Washington Junior and Senior High Schools, and East High School were the schools that many Jewish children attended in the early part of the 20th century.

*Rabbi Abraham Solomon and Temple Beth El Hebrew School. Rabbi Abraham Solomon was a very popular Hebrew School teacher. He taught at the newly organized Temple Beth El and also at his own "Cheder" on Thomas Street.*

*The text at the bottom of the photograph reads: "Yiddishah Folk Shule in 'Shlomo's Dream,' April 3, 1926. Rochester, New York. Photo by Jaffeson."*  65

# East High School
## Class of January '23

*Photos by Furlong—No. 58 Clinton avenue south*

This composite portrait of East High School's graduating class of 1923 is reproduced from the January 28, 1923 issue of Rochester's Democrat and Chronicle. *East High's 1923 graduating class included many Jewish students. Among them are Elizabeth Schwartz, former schoolteacher at School Number 8, Jack Lubell, former successful attorney, and Les Harrison, former manager of the Rochester Royals basketball team. The photos in the circular frames trace the school's initials: EHS.*

*Washington Junior High School, class of 1923.*

# Personalities

It did not take long for Jews in Rochester to become prominent citizens of the community. Jews became active in civic life as well as business and professional and Jewish organizational life. The impact of Jews in the development of the cultural, social and educational institutions of the community is far-reaching.

*Rabbi Solomon Sadowsky of Congregation Agudas Achim Nusach Ari on Morris Street became the chief orthodox rabbi in Rochester for more than a quarter of a century. Born in Russia May 25, 1879, he became a rabbi there before coming to the U.S. in 1902. He headed a congregation in Albany for eight years, and was named rabbi of Rochester's Congregation Beth Israel in 1910. In 1920 he also became rabbi of Congregation Agudas Achim Nusach Ari. Rabbi Sadowsky was an active figure in the Mizrachi Organization of America, serving as chairman of its state federation. He was a delegate to the World Zionist Congress in London in 1920 and again in Switzerland in 1937. Rabbi Sadowsky also attended the opening of Hebrew University on Mount Scopus, Palestine, in 1925. After his return, Rabbi Sadowsky was urged by a delegation from Chicago to accept the leadership position at a congregation in that city. However, he chose to remain in Rochester. He was also Jewish chaplain of the Monroe County Penitentiary and the author of three books on Jewish affairs. From the collection of Leonard Sonders.*

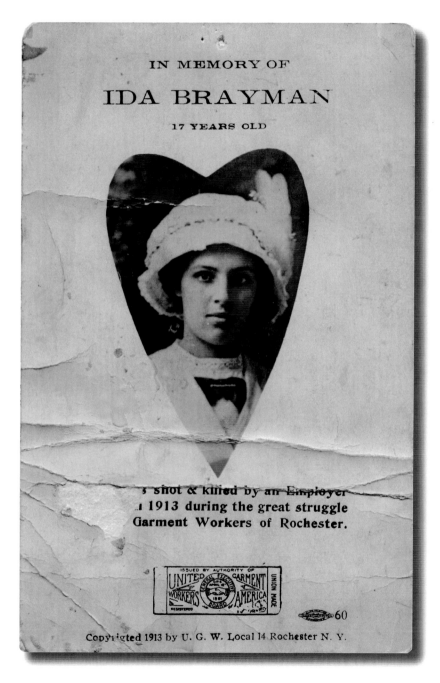

IN MEMORY OF

# IDA BRAYMAN

17 YEARS OLD

s shot & killed by an Employer
1913 during the great struggle
Garment Workers of Rochester.

Copyrigted 1913 by U. G. W. Local 14 Rochester N. Y.

*Ida Brayman, a 17-year-old worker in the garment industry in New York, came to Rochester to protest the working conditions in the clothing industry. In 1913 she was killed on Joseph Avenue during the garment workers' struggle for better working conditions in Rochester.*

*Alfred Hart took over his family grocery store business and expanded it throughout Rochester. Ultimately almost every block in the city had a Hart's Food Store. He was a noted and generous philanthropist, not only to the Jewish community but to the Greater Rochester community as well. He was instrumental in acquiring the Jewish Children's Home on Gorham Street, and later built a synagogue on its premises. He also played a major role in the formation of Temple Beth El, the first Conservative synagogue in Rochester. Upon his death his widow, Ida Hart (right), continued his philanthropic work.*

MRS. ALFRED HART . . . a lifetime of constant effort and devotion to the welfare of our people . . . a grace and warmth flowing from a great and noble heart . . . a dignity and charm reflecting an inner glow of hope and faith for our future.

\* \* \*

MRS. ELEANOR ROOSEVELT . . . the First Lady of the Free World . . . her humanitarian activities have influenced an entire generation of Americans . . . her ceaseless efforts on behalf of others have earned for her a place of esteem and honor in the history of our time.

*You are invited*
*to a Dinner on the occasion of the*
*Tenth Anniversary of Israel*
*in honor of*

*Mrs. Alfred Hart*

\* \* \*

*Guest Speaker*

*Mrs. Eleanor Roosevelt*

*Tuesday, April 29th, 1958, 6:00 p.m.*

*Temple Beth El Auditorium*

*Winton Road South*

*Rochester, New York*

*Casper L. Solomon*
General Chairman

*Leon H. Sturman*
Dinner Chairman

ROCHESTER COMMITTEE FOR STATE OF ISRAEL BONDS

*R.S.V.P.*

*$3.75 per plate*

*Invitation to Israel Bond dinner honoring Ida Hart. Mrs. Hart, the widow of Alfred Hart, a great philanthropist in Rochester, was honored in 1958 for her generosity and work for Israel Bonds. Eleanor Roosevelt was the guest speaker at the event.*

*The first Israel bonds purchased matured in 1962. Those shown above owned matured bonds.*

The booklet Higher Ideals, authored by the prominent businessman and philanthropist Alfred Hart and published in 1934, was a compendium of his thoughts concerning practical idealism in life and work.

Rabbi Abraham Solomon served as Torah reader at Temple Beth El for over 50 years. In the early years of Temple Beth El, he taught in its Hebrew school. He later established his own "Cheder" on Thomas Street.

RABBI ABRAHAM SOLOMON has been heeding the advice of Rabbi Judah for most of his 80 years. We are grateful that the Almighty has granted him the length of years, the energy, the zeal and the devotion to serve our sacred needs.

On Passover 5730, Rabbi Solomon began again the sacred round of chanting the words of the Torah for Congregation Beth El for the 51st time. He has been teacher, counselor, rabbi and friend to two generations of Rochester Jews, binding them, through his close attention to his duties, ever closer to the Jewish faith and to the Jewish people.

May the Almighty grant him, his dear life's companion, Anna, his sons and their wives and their children and their children's children the joy of each other's company in good health and in a world at peace for many more years to come.

May we of Congregation Beth El be privileged to join with the Solomon family in many more happy celebrations.

*Rabbi Philip Bernstein was chief rabbi at Temple B'rith Kodesh for many years. Rabbi Bernstein was born in Rochester in 1901 to Orthodox parents. It was under his leadership that Temple B'rith Kodesh started to move to the right, incorporating Hebrew in its services and reinstituting B'nai Mitzvot.*

*Eleanor Roosevelt became a dear friend of Rabbi Philip Bernstein.*

Rabbi Bernstein with President Lyndon Johnson in 1967. Rabbi Bernstein was not only a prominent personality in Rochester, but was recognized throughout the world as a leading Jewish figure in America. He was invited to the White House on many occasions.

*Rabbi Bernstein with General Dwight D. Eisenhower. Rabbi Bernstein became a chaplain during World War II and was stationed both in Europe and in the Pacific. After the war with Germany was over, Rabbi Bernstein stayed on to help with the displaced victims of the Holocaust.*

*Rabbi Abraham Karp served as senior rabbi of Temple Beth El for 16 years. He retired from the Rabbinate to assume the Philip Bernstein Chair of Judaic Studies at the University of Rochester. Rabbi Karp was a noted Jewish historian, collector of rare Judaic books, and author of many books on Jewish life in America, among them,* Jewish Continuity in America.

Rochester's only Jewish mayor, Sam Dicker (center, with hat and overcoat), about 1948.

Philip Liebschutz was a prominent Rochester attorney and an active leader in the Jewish as well as the general Rochester community. He was responsible for having Charles Markus bequeath his sizeable estate consisting of Kodak stock to the JY. Subsequently the JCC building on Edgewood Avenue was paid off by this donation.

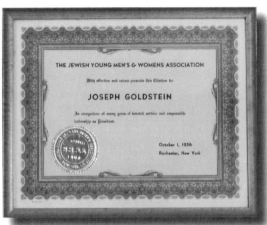

Joseph Goldstein was a prominent attorney and community leader. He served as president of the JY from 1939 to 1948. During his presidency, membership grew by leaps and bounds and the JY became the center of Jewish life in Rochester. Photo by Varden Studio.

Garson Meyer, one of the few Jews who became a Kodak executive, was very active in establishing senior adult services in Rochester.

Morris Fogel was an impressario and radio personality. Mr. Fogel was very popular among the Yiddish-speaking population of Rochester because he brought Jewish shows, popular Yiddish stars and cantors, and films (all in Yiddish) to Rochester. He was well known in Rochester for his radio program, "The Jewish Hour," which was aired every Sunday morning for at least 25 years. From the collection of Seymour Fogel.

Medals and buttons from the collection of Jack Cohen. Jack was an active member of B'nai Brith, and was instrumental in supplying furniture, religious items, etc. for Fort Ontario in Oswego, NY, a refugee camp for victims of the Holocaust. He was also an avid collector of memorabilia from the Jewish and general communities.

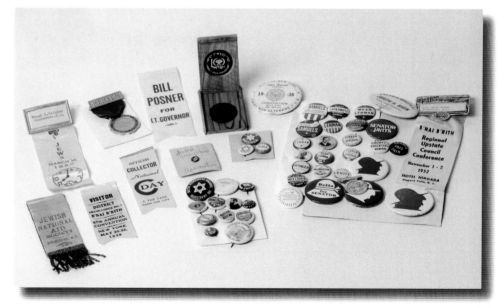

# Businesses

The clothing industry in Rochester began with the early German-Jewish immigrants. With the influx of new immigrants, the small tailor shops expanded, the industry grew, and ultimately Rochester became a manufacturing center for men's clothing. The industry was dominated by Jews and employed more workers than any other enterprise in Rochester. While the clothing manufacturers gained unrivaled prominence, they faced internal labor problems. Russian and Polish Jews came to Rochester for the opportunity of finding immediate employment in clothing factories. Working conditions were poor and wages low, causing dissatisfaction among employees. Strikes were not uncommon and disrupted the local industries. Immigrant Jewish workers were pitted against the wealthy Jewish manufacturers. As an outgrowth of the strikes and the often violent dissension, the Amalgamated Clothing Workers Union was formed not only to protect workers' rights, but also to meet many of their social service needs. Led by Abraham Chapman, it became an active and important organization in Rochester.

As the years went on, Rochester Jews were achieving success in a variety of commercial enterprises. Companies such as Rochester Knitting Works, Superba Cravats, and Shuron Optical became prominent. Retailing in Rochester was greatly influenced by the Jewish population. The National Clothing Company, led by Abraham F. Horowitz and his son Jesse, became one of Rochester's leading retail establishments. Benjamin Forman, himself an immigrant, became a tailor and ultimately established the B. Forman Company, one of the largest women's specialty shops in the country. The Neisner Brothers opened a five-and-dime store in Rochester and later expanded to many other cities. Alfred Hart's father, Moses, operated a grocery store on Hudson Avenue. Upon his father's death, Alfred took over the store. Plagued by a large overhead, he decided to open a self-service grocery on Front Street. With self-service, overhead costs were reduced and business soared. As business increased, Hart stores were opened in other neighborhoods and other towns adjacent to Rochester. The Hart stores were the forerunner to Star Supermarkets, owned and operated by Morris Levinson, Jack Rubens and their familes.

Many immigrants who started out as tailors eventually went into the retail clothing business. Others who started out as hucksters of fruits and vegetables eventually were able to open their own grocery stores, most of which were Mama and Papa stores. Some immigrants became butchers, some fishmongers, and some opened jewelry stores, hardware stores, and shoe stores. Some who peddled bread and baked goods opened their own bakeries and some of the peddlers of junk opened junkyards or went into the coal business. Most of these businesses were located in the Joseph Avenue area.

The second generation of immigrant families for the most part did not follow in their parents' footsteps by becoming laborers in the clothing industry or proprietors in family businesses. They entered professions such as medicine, accounting, pharmacy and law. This trend continued until the Jewish population of Rochester was made up of mostly professional people. Today, with the exception of the jewelry and real estate businesses, there are few Jews in the retail or clothing industries.

*Michael J. Miller, founder of Star Bottling Company.*

*Assorted soda and seltzer bottles from Star Bottling Company, Miller's Beverages, Whistle Bottling Company, and Rochester Soda Water. Rochester Soda Water Company, Inc., located on Thomas Street, bottled and sold a variety of sodas and seltzers both in the retail and wholesale markets.*

*Pee Wee soda pop distributed by Miller's Beverages. One bottle of Pee Wee sold for five cents. All the items on these two pages are from the collection of Michael Grossman.*

*Case that held 12 bottles of Miller's beverages.*

*Star Bottling Works, 35 Thomas Street.*

*Rochester Soda Water Company, Inc., owned by the Miller and Grossman families, bottled Whistle Beverages, along with many other franchised drinks. Judging by the car to the right of the Whistle Bottling Company truck, this photograph was taken in the late 1920s.*

*A. Ring & Son were popular jewelers on East Main Street.*

# August Bros. & Company

### Makers of

## Hand Tailored Clothes for Men and Young Men

187-189 St. Paul Street - Rochester, N. Y.

Among the manufacturers of Clothing in Rochester City, the city which is near the "top" when it comes to the annual output of clothing and which also enjoys the proud distinction of manufacturing more, high-grade clothing than any other city in the United States—may be noted August Bros. & Co., makers of the "Finest Ready-to-Wear," custom-made clothes.

Though young in years, this concern, which only entered the clothing manufacturing field in 1906, is rapidly forging ahead by reason of the superior designs for which the "A B C" clothing is noted.

The exclusiveness of the August Bros. clothing is due to the artistic ability of the head and founder of the business, Mr. Leo August, who prior to the establishment of the concern which bears his name, was "chief designer" and superintendent of cutters for one of the largest clothing manufactories in Rochester City, and is today recognized throughout the country as a designer of note.

Mr. Leo August founded the house of August Baum & Co., which conducted business on the site now occupied by the present firm of August Bros. & Co., but later withdrew and in connection with his brothers, Simon and David, established business at 135 and 137 St. Paul Street, locating later in their present factory building, 187-189 St. Paul St.

The August Bros. home, in which August Bros. & Co. manufacture their entire product, directly under the personal supervision of the members of the firm, is a six story structure with basement and sub-basement. The top floor of the building adjoining is also utilized.

They employ several hundred people and ship goods to all parts of the United States.

Both Messrs Simon and David August are known throughout the country as clothing salesmen, prior to entering the firm of August Bros. & Co., having been the representative of leading clothing manufacturers.

Where "A B C" Clothing is Made

LEO AUGUST

*The August Brothers and Company clothiers were located on St. Paul Street. The photograph of Leo (above) was taken in 1906.*

*The Union Outfitting Company was located on State Street.*

*Plate advertising Michael Stern Clothes. Michael Stern was one of the leading manufacturers of men's clothing in Rochester.*

*Assorted buttons, belt buckles and sewing notions from S. Kolko and Sons Tailor's Trimmings. From the collection of Anne Korenstein.*

*Charge plate from Kroll's Dress Shop, once located on Clinton Avenue near Buchan Park. Mrs. Kroll was always available to help her customers.*

*Kolko Paper Company located on the corner of Ormond Street and Kelly Street. The Kolko family ran the business for many years. From the collection of Mordecai Kolko.*

*Brodsky Textiles was a busy place, originally located on Joseph Avenue and later on Clinton Avenue between Main Street and Andrews Street. Owned by the Brodsky family, it was patronized by the entire Rochester community because its inventory of all sorts of textiles was enormous. From the collection of Eileen Brodsky Grossman.*

*Lidman's Barbershop was located on Joseph Avenue between Kelly Street and Baden Street. This photograph is from about 1920.*

*Century Printing Company, owned by Isaac, Isadore and Jacob Dworkin, 1910.*

*Toy broom manufactured by the Schwartz Broom Company. From the collection of Phyllis Kasdin.*

*The Joseph Avenue Deli located at 338 Joseph Avenue was owned by Leonard and Marion Grossman. They ran the establishment until World War II, when Leonard was called into the service. From the collection of Michael Grossman.*

*Schafer's Fish Market on Joseph Avenue near Clifford Avenue (shown here circa 1930) was a popular place to purchase fresh fish. Sam Schafer and his family worked in the market until one Sunday in the 1960s a burglar entered the store and gouged out Sam Schafer's eyes. From the collection of Ruth Lempert.*

*Rebecca Bogorad at the family hot dog stand in Charlotte, circa 1925. The Bogorad family operated many hot dog stands, among them stands at Sea Breeze and in Charlotte.*

*Cohen's Kosher Restaurant on Joseph Avenue became an institution in the Rochester Jewish community. Featured in this late 1920s photograph are (behind the counter) Mrs. Cohen, Mr. Cohen and Jack Cohen. Jack carried on the family business until 1965. He attempted to rebuild the business after the riots, but found it too dangerous to remain on Joseph Avenue.*

An advertisement for Applebaum's kosher meat market on Joseph Avenue, owned by Sarah and Isadore P. (also known as Philip) Applebaum. When he was young, Philip was a newspaper carrier, and his newsboy badge is pictured below.

Above: Sour cream jars from Polsky's Dairy, Cloverdale Dairy, Sunny Farms Dairy, and Danishefsky's Creamery. Below: Assorted milk bottles from Newman's Dairy, Hudson Dairy, and Cami Dairy. From the collection of Albert Newman.

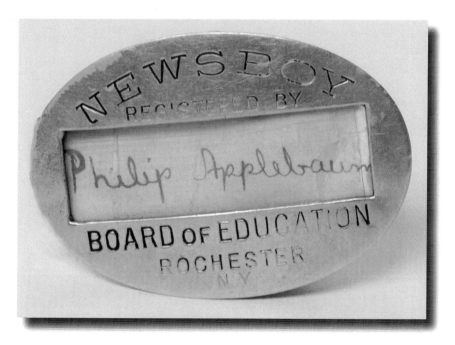

Sam Weinstein and his son Morris (lower left) repair bicycles at 825 North Clinton Avenue (upper right). Sam Weinstein first opened a shop in the garage behind his mother's house on Scrantom Street in the 1930s. As his business grew, he moved to North Clinton Avenue, where the store thrived until it closed in the late 1970s. Sam's children, Seymour, Morrie and Lois (lower right), learned to run the business at an early age. Every weekend they rented bikes at Sam's Scottsville Road store. From the collection of the Weinstein family—Lois DeCoste and Morrie and Seymour Weinstein.

*The Germanow-Simon Machine Company was founded by Julius Simon (left) and Harry Germanow (right) in 1916. It has remained a family business through the years and is now known as the Germanow-Simon Corporation, manufacturing dial thermometers, plastic optics, and precision tools for watchmakers, jewelers and hobbyists. Today the company's CEO and president is Andrew Germanow, following in the footsteps of his grandfather, Harry, father, Irving, and uncle Leon. Leonard Simon, Julius Simon's son, is chairman of the board. Photo courtesy of the Germanow-Simon Corporation.*

*Jewish businesses advertised in the programs for JY dances
and in other publications.*

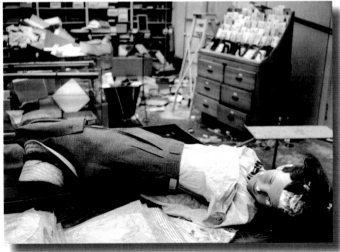

*Itkin's Department Store catered mostly to the residents of the Joseph Avenue area. Owned and operated by the Itkins, it was a thriving business until the civil riots of 1964, when the store was ransacked and nearly destroyed.*

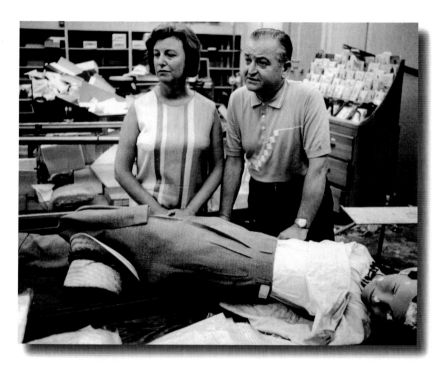

*Diane and Meyer Rock were devastated as they surveyed the remains of their clothing store after the riots. The photographs on these two pages are from the collection of Diane Rock, courtesy of Life magazine.*

# Neighborhoods

The earliest German Jewish immigrants settled primarily in the Main Street/Front Street area. As business improved they moved to the Joseph Avenue area, mainly Chatham (later renamed Ormond Street), Joiner, Oregon, and Nassau Streets. Following the Civil War, a steady exodus from the older Jewish neighborhoods began. In the 1870s they moved to Franklin Park, North and South Street (today the downtown area), and as far south as South Union Street. By the mid-1880s the newer sections near Arnold Park, Nichols Park (today Oxford Street), East Avenue, and North Goodman Street became the residences of the wealthier Jews.

As the Russian, Polish and Sephardic Jews became Americanized and somewhat affluent, they, too, migrated away from the Joseph Avenue area. They took up residence to the North in the St. Paul Street/Conkey Avenue area and eventually north of Ridge Road in Irondequoit. Other, more affluent Jews moved south to the Park Avenue/Monroe Avenue sections of town, eventually migrating to Brighton and, more recently, to Pittsford. After World War II, in the late 1940s and into the 1950s, Holocaust survivors, or refugees, as they were called, started to come to Rochester. Just as earlier immigrants settled in the Joseph Avenue area, these newly arrived refugees settled in the same area. It did not take long, however, for them to accumulate enough resources so that they could move to a better neighborhood.

The old Jewish Section of the Joseph Avenue area is gone. Urban Renewal eliminated many of the streets. In their stead, low income housing was erected. The synagogues were demolished, as were some of the businesses. The riots in 1964 became the impetus for the demise of Jewish Joseph Avenue. Some businesses stayed in the area after the riots, but it didn't take long for them to close because it was too dangerous to remain open. The only vestige today of Jewish life on Joseph Avenue is one synagogue, Congregation B'nai Israel.

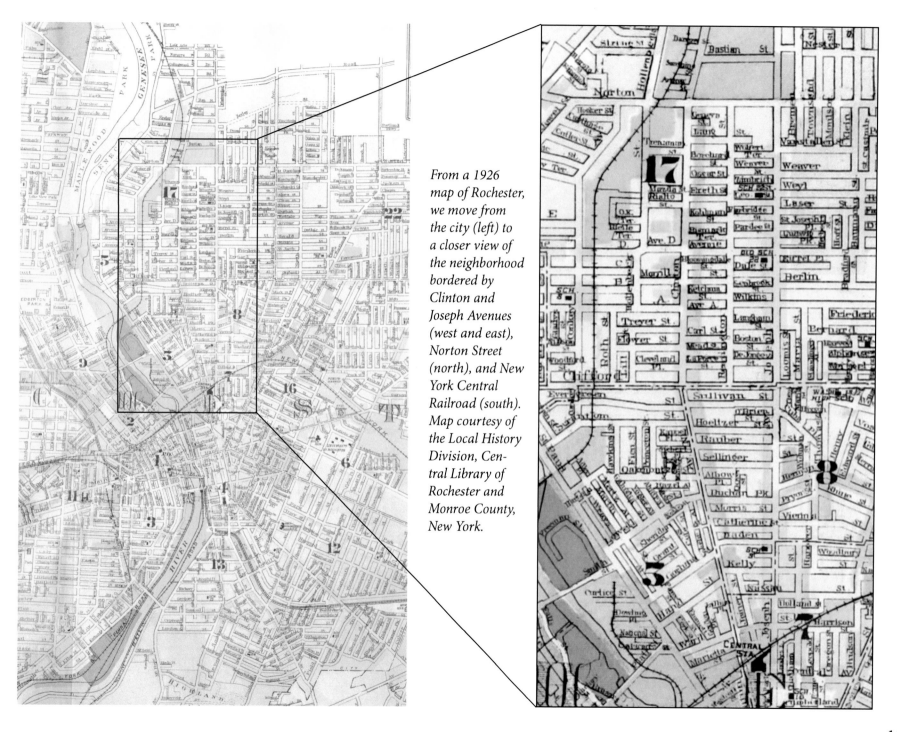

From a 1926 map of Rochester, we move from the city (left) to a closer view of the neighborhood bordered by Clinton and Joseph Avenues (west and east), Norton Street (north), and New York Central Railroad (south). Map courtesy of the Local History Division, Central Library of Rochester and Monroe County, New York.

**Marcia Schafer Ostroff:** *When the iceman with his horse and wagon stopped at my father's store to deliver ice, I scooped up the chips that flew off the block of ice that the iceman was cutting so I could suck on the cold slivers.*

**Leon Berman:** *Living in the Joseph Avenue area was comfortable because all the kids were in the same economic level— POOR!*

*Ormand Street facing Baden Street. Ormond Street, formerly Chatham Street, consisted mainly of synagogues, businesses and some residences. The view toward Baden Street shows Danishefsky's Creamery and Al's Market, formerly Lifschutz's grocery store.*

108 Neighborhoods

*Joseph Avenue at Vienna Street during the 1950s. Though Jewish businesses were still doing well on Joseph Avenue, most of the residents had already moved away.*

**Rita Rudnick:**
*My memories of Joseph Avenue are mainly Brodsky's and the New York Bakery. My mother was a seamstress and would take me to Brodsky's but would be constantly looking at fabrics and would forget me, so I just climbed around the empty shelves until it was time to leave.*

**Al Kasdin:**
*After work at Byer's Shoe Store, I'd stop by for a hot salami sandwich at Cohen's. Boy, were they good!*

109

**Annette Itkin:**

*Itkin's Department store and many of the Joseph Avenue businesses were open during the Depression. All the merchants were like family as they helped each other financially and all survived. Itkin's Department Store's motto was: "It-kin be had for less at Itkin's."*

**Ann Friedman Roth:**

*It was a fun time. People came from all over the city to shop on Saturday night. It was like a party!*

**Libby Lavner:**

*I remember sitting on my Mother's porch on Rhine Street on the High Holy Days and watching the people in their new outfits walk to shul. It was quite a sight to see. We had a shul on our street.*

**Tillie Levinson:**

*Morris Street was my residence. I was the shopper in my family and I fondly recall all the wonderful stores on Joseph Avenue, among them bakeries, creameries, and meat markets.*

**Daniel Lempert:**

*We lived near Morgan's Barn where the work horses for the city were kept and used for street cleaning, plowing, and garbage collecting, so I shouldn't have been surprised when my mother awoke one morning to find a horse looking at her through her bedroom window, as if to say, "Do you have any hay?"*

**Jerry Veiner:**

*I remember wooden barrels of pickles and herring. "Nickel a Shtickel" hunks of salami at Fox's. The first time I saw television was probably 1947 or 1948 at Rocky's Bookie establishment.*

**Gilbert Cresov:**

*My fondest memory of living in the Joseph Avenue area is walking with my father on Sunday mornings as he shopped. We stopped at Appelbaum's Meat Market where we bought homemade rolled beef. Mr. Appelbaum always gave me a slice. Our next stop was the New York Bakery for rye bread and a Danish which we split and ate as we walked. We did not own a car. Last stop was Rocky's Hobby Shop. My father and Rocky were stamp collectors. They talked about stamps as my father slipped him some money to bet on a baseball game.*

*Though few residences remained in the Main Street/Front Street area around the turn of the century, many Jewish businesses in the area were still open. This photo was taken in front of the Manson News Agency on Front Street during the Flood of 1913. It was made into a postcard (the back of which is to the right), and was sent from "Dave" in Rochester to Mr. Joe Epstein in Watertown, NY, on April 4, 1913.*

*Morrie Silver (1908–1974), right, is credited with saving Rochester's Red Wings baseball team in 1956 when the St. Louis Cardinals announced their intention to abandon the Rochester franchise. He devised a plan to sell shares of stock to local citizens, and in less than a week raised $294,000. The Red Wings' stadium on Norton Street, built in 1929, was renamed Silver Stadium in 1968 in honor of Morrie Silver, and the team played there until Frontier Field replaced it in 1997. The photograph of Silver Stadium above was taken on October 9, 1996 for Rochester Institute of Technology's tenth annual Big Shot. The temperature outside was 45 degrees Fahrenheit, the exposure was 1.5 minutes, and all external lighting was provided by multiple flashes of electronic flash units operated by 125 people. The "baseball players" on the field are RIT students wearing original Red Wings uniforms. Photo of Morrie Silver from the collection of Naomi Silver and the Rochester Red Wings archives.*

# Final Thoughts

Today the population of the Rochester Jewish community is around 20,000. It is an active and vibrant community that is recognized with high regard by the general community. Currently there are five Orthodox congregations, four Conservative congregations, four Reform congregations and one Humanistic congregation. The Jewish Federation is the central fund-raising, planning, and community relations organization for the Rochester Jewish community. Under its umbrella are the JCC, the Jewish Home of Rochester, Jewish Family Service, Hillel School, and the Hillel Foundation. Many other Jewish philanthropic organizations are also organized and run by very dedicated volunteers. We've come a long way since the first German Jews settled in this city. It is our hope that future generations will print a sequel to this volume memorializing the accomplishments of the Rochester Jewish community during the end of the 20th century and the 21st century. Indeed, the future begins with the past.

*The newest wing of the JCC complex at 1200 Edgewood Avenue is the Wolk Children's Center, an environment carefully planned for the young child. Photo by Frank Cost.*

# Inspiring Jewish Journeys

Nearly 100 years ago, when the 21$^{st}$ century was only spoken of in science fiction books, members of Rochester's Jewish community came together to create an institution that would outlive them all. The founders of the Jewish Young Men's and Women's Association (JY) have left a legacy with an impact more valuable to our community than even they could have envisioned at the time.

Beginning with our first home on Franklin Square in 1907, and moving to the Andrews Street Building in the 1930s, and finally to Edgewood Avenue in 1973, the story of the JY/JCC is a testimonial to the commitment of a generation of Jews to thrive and flourish in what was, for many of them, a new country.

The Jewish Community Center of today embodies a proud and exciting history. It would be a dififcult task, indeed, to find a Jewish family in Rochester that has no past or present connection to the JCC. By design and need, the JCC has grown into the busiest Jewish neighborhood in Rochester. It is a place where Jews and non-Jews of all ages and backgrounds, affiliations and practices, come together, to learn, play, connect to each other, and grow.

The JCC has become the educational, social, cultural and recreational center of the Jewish community. We strive to inspire Jewish journeys in myriad ways. The production and publication of this beautiful book is intended to be an inspiration to all of us as, through its pages, we follow the journey of our extended Jewish family.

My heartfelt thanks and appreciation to Phyllis Kasdin who conceived the idea for the archives exhibit; to all of the volunteers who helped to mount the original exhibit; to Michael Peres for sharing his amazing skill and talent as a photographer; to Frank and Patricia Cost, our extremely professional and creative book designers; and to our very special and generous underwriters who believed this was an important project to support.

To our community—I sincerely hope that this book represents a meaningful mile marker in your individual Jewish journeys.

**Leslie Berkowitz**
*Executive Director*
*Jewish Community Center*
*of Greater Rochester*

# Production Notes

The idea for producing this book, *The Future Begins with the Past*, was presented to us in February 2005. As Phyllis Kasdin explains in the Preface, most of these photographs and family heirlooms came from an exhibition at the Jewish Community Center. More than 300 family treasures from the local Jewish community were included. Because of the show, single pictures became part of a larger collection of Rochester's Jewish past that begged to be preserved in some way.

The images on the pages of this book are the result of years of preserving "shoeboxes of pictures" by families and organizations. The photographs of the revered Rabbi Sadowsky from the early 1900s and the Whistle Bottling Company's delivery truck drivers, for example, were probably kept in boxes for years and seen by only a few people on special occasions in the privacy of their homes. Shoeboxes are well-suited for storing photographs because they are small, dry, and provide a safe space for small items, but the contents of private shoeboxes remain hidden from public view.

Most of the photographs from the exhibit now reside in the JCC's photo archives collection. We received the photographs selected for this book in various states of preserve. Many of our "originals" were actually copies of the original photographs; some of the actual original photographs we received had deteriorated considerably over the years; and other original photographs appeared as pristine as they must have been on the day of their creation.

Each photograph tells a story, but how each piece has existed until today is also a story. Many of the pictures reproduced here were passed from generation to generation or traveled through many hands. After poring over this collection for the past few months, we

*Several of the "original" photographs we used to produce this book were already reproductions. One example is this section of a collage made up of newspaper clippings and other reproduced photographs that was presented to Alfred Hart from the residents, staff and board of directors of the Jewish Children's Home on Gorham Street.*

are tempted to ask who made the original photographs and why. The majority of the photographs seem to have been taken to document or promote various Jewish organizations and institutions, and so production details about the photographs were not recorded.

Every effort was made to reach the copyright holders of the original photographs reproduced in this book. The Center requested and received permission from all the owners of the photographs and heirlooms pictured here, however in most cases the identity of the original photographer could not be determined.

In some cases it was easy to learn who made a picture, such as the work of Mr. S. Stanton Singer from 1931, because his stamp is prominently displayed on the back of his photograph (see below). However, with most of the others, there was no such information.

Pictures have become so common that we often overlook their power and ability to preserve the past in meaningful ways. They evoke memories and remind us of where we come from. This book is filled with wonderful photographs and memorabilia chronicling the Rochester Jewish community's history, spanning a period of more than 90 years. We sincerely appreciate the trust that the Jewish Community Center had in us to produce it, and we hope its reception in the community is as satisfying as the process of creating it has been for us.

Michael Peres
Professor
Rochester Institute of Technology

Frank Cost
Professor
Rochester Institute of Technology

Patricia Cost
Publisher
Fossil Press

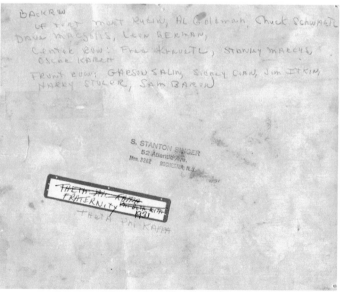

*Front and back of the cast photograph of Theta Phi Kappa's 1931 operetta in drag, with S. Stanton Singer's stamp prominently diplayed on the back.*

# Credits

All reproductions in this book of both artifacts and original images are by Michael Peres. Other credits are listed here.

107     1926 map of Joseph Ave. area
        *Plat Book of the City of Rochester, New York*
        G.M. Hopkins, publisher, Philadephia
        courtesy of Larry Naukaum, Local History Division,
        Central Library of Rochester and Monroe County, New York

112     RIT Big Shot #10, Silver Stadium, 1996
        produced by Rochester Red Wings Baseball Club,
        Rochester Institute of Technology, and RIT's
        School of Photographic Arts and Sciences

112     Morrie Silver standing in Silver Stadium
        from the collection of Naomi Silver and
        the Rochester Red Wings archives

113     Wolk Children's Center
        photo by Frank Cost

115     Theta Phi Kappa cast
        photo by S. Stanton Singer
        52 Atlantic Avenue, Rochester

# Underwriters

We are most grateful to our underwriters for their support and generosity, and for making this book possible.

The Joseph and Anna Gartner Foundation Philanthropic Fund (Carol and Michael Hirsch)

The Brodsky-Grossman Supporting Foundation, Inc. (Alan Brodsky, Eileen and Michael Grossman, Betsey and Marc Haas, and Lisa and Andrew Curwin)

The Stephen Rosenberg Memorial Fund (Haskell, Sunny and Nellie Rosenberg)

Seymour Fogel

Josephine and Simon Braitman

# Fossil Press

We are a private press devoted to producing documentary work that will gain value with the passing of time.